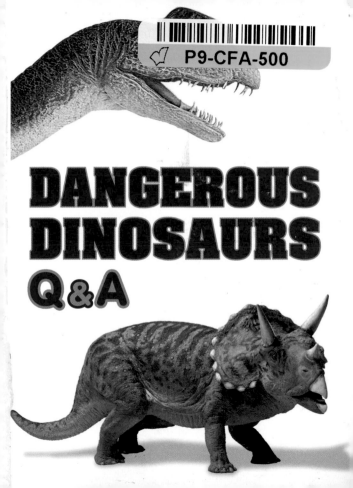

DANGEROUS DINOSAURS
Q&A

DANGEROUS

DINOSAURS
Q&A

WRITTEN BY **CAREY SCOTT**
CONSULTANT **DAVID LAMBERT**

Content previously published in a larger format

LONDON, NEW YORK,
MELBOURNE, MUNICH, AND DELHI

THIS NEW EDITION
Senior Editor Shannon Beatty
Designer Jessica Park
Editorial Director Nancy Ellwood

ORIGINAL EDITION
Senior Art Editor Smiljka Surla
Senior Editor Fran Jones
Managing Editor Linda Esposito
Managing Art Editor Diane Thistlethwaite
Publishing Manager Andrew Macintyre
Category Publisher Laura Buller
Design Development Manager Sophia
M. Tampakopoulos
Production Editor Hitesh Patel
DK Picture Library Claire Bowers
Jacket Editor Mariza O'Keeffe
Jacket Designers Sophia M.
Tampakopoulos, Natasha Rees

First American edition, 2008

This edition, 2012

Published in the United States by
DK Publishing
375 Hudson Street
New York, New York 10014

12 13 14 15 16 10 9 8 7 6 5 4 3 2 1

001—187220—July/2012

Published in Great Britain by Dorling
Kindersley Limited.

A catalog record for this book is available
from the Library of Congress.

ISBN 978–0–7566–9252–0

DK books are available at special discounts
when purchased in bulk for sales
promotions, premiums, fund-raising, or
educational use. For details, contact: DK
Publishing Special Markets, 375 Hudson
Street, New York, New York 10014 or
SpecialSales@dk.com.

Printed and bound in China by South China

Discover more at
www.dk.com

CONTENTS

AGE OF T -

WHAT IS A
dinosaur?

Dinosaurs were land-dwelling reptiles with long tails, clawed hands and feet, and scaly skin. Some walked on two legs, others on four. While some were meat-eaters, others munched on plants. Most people know what a dinosaur looks like from books and movies. But even experts are still unsure why dinosaurs survived when their rivals died out. It was probably their erect stance, the sheer size of the largest, such as *Giganotosaurus*, and their efficient weapons of attack and defense that ensured their long-lasting success.

GIGANOTOSAURUS

Long tail used for balance

Most meat-eaters had three clawed fingers on each hand

Large, clawed, birdlike feet

In what way were dinosaurs different?

Dinosaurs were different from other reptiles because they could stand with their legs straight. Most reptiles have legs that splay out from their bodies, giving them a sprawling stance. Dinosaurs were like mammals—they could walk upright with their legs directly beneath them.

BAROSAURUS

WAS *EORAPTOR* THE FIRST OF THE DINOSAURS?

It was certainly one of the earliest dinosaurs. The remains of *Eoraptor*—a small, meat-eating dinosaur—were discovered in 1991 in South America, where dinosaurs may have originated. Experts estimate that *Eoraptor* was alive and well as long as 228 million years ago.

EORAPTOR

Five-fingered hands with weaker claws than later species

VELOCIRAPTOR

Were dinosaurs warm-blooded?

No one is sure. Reptiles such as snakes are cold-blooded, which means that their body temperature cools down with the outside temperature and they become less active. But evidence suggests that some dinosaurs,

such as *Velociraptor*, had feathers, and feathered animals are warm-blooded. Some experts now believe that all the dinosaurs may have been warm-blooded, enabling them to be active whatever the weather.

Did dinosaurs have
CLAWS?

All dinosaurs had clawed feet and hands. Some claws were like the talons of birds of prey, while others resembled curved, sharp scissors. They were either used to pull high branches down for food or to slash live prey or stab at attackers. Some "claws" were more like the hooves of cattle and merely acted to protect the toes.

BONES OF
TYRANNOSAURUS FOOT

Wing
membrane •

Were there dinosaurs that could fly?

Dinosaurs were all land-dwelling animals. But there were plenty of flying creatures in the prehistoric skies, and they were reptiles, just like the dinosaurs. They were called pterosaurs, which means "winged lizard." There were many different types of pterosaur, some as big as light aircraft. *Rhamphorhynchus* was over 3 ft (1 m) long with a narrow jaw and pointed teeth for catching fish.

The remains of this dinosaur's last meal—a lizardlike animal—are still in its stomach

COELOPHYSIS

How do we know about them?

Everything we know about dinosaurs comes from scientific evidence. That means the real, physical remains of the animals that have been preserved in the world's deserts, riverbeds, and cliffs for millions and millions of years. It was not until the 19th century that the remains were correctly identified and the science of paleontology was born. Since then, amazing discoveries have been made worldwide, including this complete skeleton of *Coelophysis*, unearthed in the sands of Texas.

What is a fossil?

AMMONITE

A fossil is the preserved remains of a plant or animal. These remains can be either hardened bones, shells, or other parts, or a preserved impression of the hard parts. One of the most common fossils is an ammonite—a shelled sea creature that lived at the same time as the dinosaurs.

WHEN WERE DINOSAURS FIRST IDENTIFIED?

MEGALOSAURUS JAW

1842

People have been collecting dinosaur fossils for many years, but it was not until 1842 that dinosaurs were recognized as a distinct group of animals. When this jaw was found in England, experts realized that this, and other remains, belonged to extinct giant reptiles. Soon the term "dinosaur" was used to describe them.

What is a
paleontologist?

Paleontologists are those scientists who study
fossils. They work both at the world's fossil
sites, excavating fossils, and in the laboratory,
cleaning and analyzing fossils. Here, a
paleontologist treats a sauropod bone before
moving it from the Sahara Desert. Dinosaur
bones are easily uncovered in the desert sands
without the need to dig deep.

HOW IS A DINOSAUR SKELETON MADE?

People often think that dinosaur skeletons in museums are real, but they are usually replicas. Paleontologists create a complete skeleton from synthetic bones, using a few fossilized bones and skeletons of dinosaur relatives as a guide. Some skeletons are made from a mix of fossilized and synthetic bones.

Two rows of pointed plates along spine

TUOJIANGOSAURUS

Spiked tail

The horns give this dinosaur its name •

TRICERATOPS

How do dinosaurs get their names?

Many dinosaurs are named after a distinguishing feature. For example, *Triceratops* means "three-horned face." Some are named because of where they were found—*Argentinosaurus* is a "reptile of Argentina." Others are called after the person who discovered them: *Herrerasaurus* means "Herrera's reptile."

HOW LONG DID DINOSAURS RULE?

Dinosaurs stomped their way across the Earth for about 160 million years and were the dominant land animals for 143 million years. During this huge stretch of time (humans have been around for less than 2 million years), many species became extinct but others evolved to take their place. Dinosaurs were survivors and most were able to adapt to their ever-changing world. *Dilophosaurus*, although not the largest of dinosaurs, was a meat-eater from the Jurassic Period. The last dinosaur expired 65 million years ago.

Muscular neck

DILOPHOSAURUS

Three claws on hand

Long, slim legs and feet

WHO RULED BEFORE THE DINOSAURS?

Before the age of the dinosaurs, the land was dominated by a group of animals that were neither reptiles nor mammals. The therapsids included this *Lystrosaurus*, a stocky, tusked plant-eater, about the size of a sheep. Most were extinct by 200 million years ago, when the dinosaurs grew dominant, although no one knows if they were wiped out by the dinosaurs.

LYSTROSAURUS

PLATEOSAURUS

WHY DO SPECIES DIE OUT?

All living things die, and all species eventually become extinct. Most individual species of dinosaur existed for about 2–3 million years. Some species evolved into different ones by adapting to changing habitats, while others were unable to adapt. Some, such as *Plateosaurus*, may have died out because of a violent change to the environment that wiped out many animals.

Did dinosaurs ever get sick?

Since the main dinosaur evidence is their bones, the only diseases that experts have found are those that affect the bones. This section of a dinosaur's backbone shows a tumor that may have been caused by cancer. Although it cannot be scientifically proved, it is likely that dinosaurs suffered from infectious diseases, just as animals do today.

Lump on the vertebra, possibly caused by cancer

SECTION OF BACKBONE

VELOCIRAPTOR
ATTACKING *PROTOCERATOPS*

How many groups existed together?

Many dinosaur species became extinct while new species evolved over the long period of dinosaur rule, so many species did not coexist. Even so, dozens or even hundreds of different species did live at the same time in the same area. Experts know that *Velociraptor* was around at the same time as *Protoceratops*, because fossilized bones of the two have been discovered locked in battle.

HOW LONG DID A DINOSAUR USUALLY LIVE?

Bigger animals usually have a longer lifespan than small ones, so it is likely that the big plant-eating dinosaurs lived the longest. If one of these had a lucky life, it may have survived for 200 years or more. However, most dinosaurs would have died from accidents, starvation, or illness long before they could reach old age.

MODEL OF *BARYONYX*

When did dinosaurs live?

1. The first dinosaurs, such as Eoraptor and Herrerasaurus, appeared in the mid Triassic Period.

HERRERASAURUS

TRIASSIC

2. The Jurassic Period was dominated by the giant plant-eaters. Plated dinosaurs, such as the stegosaurs, appeared then, too.

DILOPHOSAURUS

LESOTHOSAURUS

ANCHISAURUS

JURASSIC

3. The dinosaurs were at their height in the Cretaceous Period. Some grew horns and frills, others developed club tails, and some refined their killing instincts.

BARYONYX

IGUANODON

CRETACEOUS

Our planet Earth was probably formed about 4.5 billion years ago, and the first animal life appeared about 1 billion years ago. The age when dinosaurs lived, from 251–65 million years ago (mya), is called the Mesozoic Era, and scientists divide this into three periods—Triassic, Jurassic, and Cretaceous.

251 MILLION YEARS AGO (MYA)

STEGOSAURUS

ARCHAEOPTERYX

BAROSAURUS

200 MYA

CORYTHOSAURUS

TRICERATOPS

DEINONYCHUS

EUOPLOCEPHALUS

145 MYA – 65 MYA

27

Were all dinosaurs
THE SAME?

No, they were not. There were lumbering animals as big as buses. There were long-necked giants as tall as trees. There were massive predators that none could challenge. And darting around their feet were nimble chicken-sized dinosaurs. Some dinosaurs were numerous; others were rare. Some were plated, frilled, or horned; others were merely weird looking. *Chindesaurus*, shown here, was a carnivorous dinosaur that lived during the late Triassic Period.

CHINDESAURUS

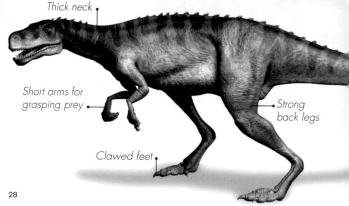

Thick neck

Short arms for
grasping prey

Strong
back legs

Clawed feet

What are the two main types of dinosaur?

The first dinosaurs evolved into two different types, or orders, based on the shape of the hip bones. Ornithischians were bird-hipped and saurischians were lizard-hipped. The two orders gave rise to different families made up of genera. More than 540 different genera have been described so far.

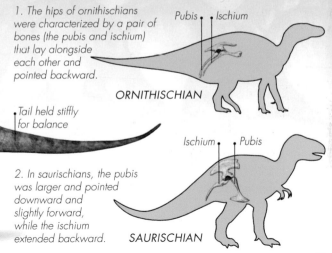

1. The hips of ornithischians were characterized by a pair of bones (the pubis and ischium) that lay alongside each other and pointed backward.

Pubis Ischium

ORNITHISCHIAN

Tail held stiffly for balance

Ischium Pubis

2. In saurischians, the pubis was larger and pointed downward and slightly forward, while the ischium extended backward.

SAURISCHIAN

PANGAEA

TETHYS SEA

PANGAEA

TRIASSIC
EARTH

Dinosaurs lived in every part of the globe. However, when they first appeared, the world's land was a giant continent, known as Pangaea, which formed a C-shape around the Tethys Sea. Later, the landmass broke up into smaller continents. Dinosaur fossils have been found as far south as Antarctica, which was not covered with snow at that time.

Which was the most common dinosaur?

Experts can only estimate the answer to this question based on the numbers of fossil finds. So many skulls of *Protoceratops* have been found in the Gobi Desert that the dinosaur is sometimes called the "sheep of the Gobi." In North America, the remains of entire herds of duck-billed or hadrosaur dinosaurs have been unearthed.

Neck frill

PROTOCERATOPS

WERE THERE ANY
mammals?

Mammals evolved around the same time as the dinosaurs, so the two animal groups coexisted. But mammals were unable to compete with dinosaurs in size or ferocity, and throughout the Mesozoic Era most were small, shrewlike animals. Many, like this *Eozostrodon*, hunted at night to avoid meat-eating dinosaurs. They fed on insects and other small animals.

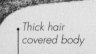

Thick hair covered body

EOZOSTRODON

THERIZINOSAURUS

Covering of feathers •

WHICH WAS THE weirdest DINOSAUR?

During the 1940s, paleontologists on fossil hunts in Mongolia made some unusual finds— giant claws over 3 ft (1 m) long, as well as parts of limbs. Some time later a skeleton was pieced together. What it revealed was a dinosaur like no other: two-legged, 36 ft (11 m) tall, with 8 ft- (2.5 m-) long arms ending in enormous claws, and probably covered with downy feathers. The weird find was named *Therizinosaurus*, meaning "scythe lizard."

Clawed feet •

HOW WAS A
DINOSAUR BORN?

Dinosaurs did not give birth to live young in the way that mammals do. Like most reptiles, and like birds, female dinosaurs laid a number of eggs. These eggs were usually deposited in a nest made of twigs and leaves, or in a hole that the female had dug in the soil or sand. Dinosaur eggs could be oval or round and as small as a tennis ball or as large as a cannonball. A baby dinosaur, such as this *Troodon*, may have pecked its way out of its protective shell with a specially designed egg tooth, just as baby birds do.

TROODON

Teeth and claws were not yet developed enough for the hatched baby to catch its own food

How many **eggs** did a dinosaur lay?

Some dinosaurs laid about 20 eggs and carefully arranged them in a circle inside the nest. Female sauropods may have laid up to 40 eggs. It is likely that dinosaurs laid eggs once a year, so a single female dinosaur probably hatched hundreds of babies in her lifetime. Experts think that between 50–90 percent of eggs survived to hatching.

OVIRAPTOR

What was the **BIGGEST** egg?

Not surprisingly the biggest dinosaurs—the plant-eating sauropods—laid some of the biggest eggs, although these were surprisingly small. A sauropod egg weighed about 11 lb (5 kg) and was about 12 in (30 cm) long. This is only about twice the size of an ostrich egg, and tiny compared to the size of the mother.

SAUROPOD EGGS

OVIRAPTOR ON
ITS NEST

Eggs in nest

Did females sit on their nests?

This 80 million-year-old fossilized *Oviraptor* nest proved
to be an amazing discovery. The mother *Oviraptor* had
died with her arms spread over her eggs, as if protecting
them. This suggests that *Oviraptor*, and probably other
birdlike dinosaurs, were brooders—they sat on their nests
to keep the eggs warm or cool.

37

DID DINOSAURS LOOK AFTER THEIR YOUNG?

Fossil evidence suggests that a female *Maiasaura* brought food to her babies after hatching, and may even have looked after her young for up to a year. There is no evidence that other dinosaurs cared for live young, but it is likely that many stayed near the nest to guard their eggs, like their closest living relatives, crocodiles.

YOUNG *MAIASAURA* WITH MOTHER

HOW FAST DID BABIES GROW?

★ ★ ★ ★ ★ ★ ★ ★ ★ ★ ★ ★ ★ ★

After hatching, dinosaur babies, like these *Troodons*, grew quickly—most had to learn to defend themselves fast if they were to survive. Fossil evidence of hadrosaur young shows that they doubled in size in about six weeks. A one-year-old *Maiasaura* was about 10 ft (3 m) long. Depending on their type, dinosaurs were generally fully grown after about 14 years.

SCAVENGERS

Muscular neck

Strong thigh bone

Short arms

Heart

Strong leg muscles

CARNOTAURUS

Powerful legs

Three-toed feet

WHAT IS A
THEROPOD?

Put simply, a theropod was a flesh-eating dinosaur. This lizard-hipped group of dinosaurs included some of the largest carnivores ever to roam the Earth. Although theropods often had wimpy arms, they did have strong muscles to power their rear legs. They also had large teeth and strong jaws. Most, such as *Carnotaurus*, had three-toed feet ending in claws. Not all theropods were huge— some were as small as chickens and survived by snapping up lizards and maybe insects.

How **BIG** were a killer's teeth?

MEGALOSAURUS
TOOTH

HUMAN
TOOTH

Carnivore fossils generally show curved, daggerlike teeth that would have sliced prey to shreds. The size of the tooth was generally a guide to the size of the animal and could be up to 8 in (20 cm) long. This tooth, which is 4 in (9 cm) long, comes from the mouth of *Megalosaurus*—a large theropod from the Jurassic Period.

WHAT DOES BIPEDAL MEAN?

TYRANNOSAURUS CLAWED FEET

A bipedal animal is one that walks on two legs. All the meat-eating dinosaurs were bipedal, although there were some plant-eaters that also walked on two legs. Bipedal dinosaurs were faster and mostly more intelligent than their four-legged cousins. The first dinosaurs, such as *Eoraptor*, were bipedal, as were some of the later ones, such as *T. rex*.

COULD A **CARNIVORE EAT A** PLANT-EATER?

A big hunter, such as *Allosaurus*, would have had several advantages over lumbering plant-eater *Stegosaurus*. Not only was *Allosaurus* faster and more quick-witted, but it was also better equipped for killing. *Allosaurus* could slash out with its claws before sinking its razor-sharp teeth into its victim's flesh. *Stegosaurus* might have fought back by swiping out with its tail spikes, but that was unlikely to prevent it from ending up as food for its killer.

ALLOSAURUS

STEGOSAURUS

HOW DID A THEROPOD RUN?

1. Albertosaurus ran with a horizontal back, head held high, and its body balanced by its stiff tail.

2. Three walking toes spread on the ground for stability as the second leg was lifted.

A dinosaur's fossilized bones and joints provide clues about how the animal moved. For example, paleontologists can figure out how far the limbs could reach. Large thigh bones indicate strong, muscular thighs, and long shin and foot bones suggest that the dinosaur was a fast runner.

3. When off the ground, the toes bunched together to minimize air resistance and increase speed.

WHICH DINOSAUR HAD THE BIGGEST BRAIN?

TROODON

The dinosaur with the biggest brain was probably *Giganotosaurus*, although this was definitely not the smartest. That honor goes to the troodontid group, which had the biggest brains for their size. These dinosaurs also had large, foward-facing eyes that could focus on prey and may have helped *Troodon* to see at night.

WHO HUNTED THE HUNTERS?

It is possible that the big carnivores—*Allosaurus*, *T. rex*, and *Giganotosaurus*—hunted smaller carnivores, such as *Santanaraptor*, as well as herbivorous dinosaurs. These big carnivores were the largest, fiercest animals around, which made them top predators, safe from hunters themselves. Only a severe wound or debilitating illness could have made a big carnivore potential prey.

SANTANARAPTOR

DEINONYCHUS ATTACKING *TENONTOSAURUS*

How did hunters *kill* their prey?

The predatory dinosaurs had to kill to stay alive, and they developed different methods and weapons for efficient hunting. Once they had moved in for the kill, they would have used teeth, claws, and powerful jaws to dispatch their victims. Small carnivores generally relied on speed and agility to capture their prey, but when the target was a big dinosaur, such as *Tenontosaurus*, they may have attacked in packs.

Did *Deinonychus* have
killer claws?

This hunter wielded a large, sickle-shaped claw on the second toe of each foot. Experts think that *Deinonychus* held its prey with its hands and jaws, and slashed at its victim with one razor-sharp claw until the unfortunate creature was dead.

Curved claw hooked the prey

Killer claw was flicked forward into victim's flesh

DEINONYCHUS CLAW

DID HUNTERS
STALK
THEIR PREY?

The more intelligent predatory dinosaurs may have stalked their prey, waiting to pounce in a moment of weakness. A lone herbivore, such as this *Iguanodon*, would have been at risk from stalkers such as *Neovenator*. To attack a dinosaur in a herd, the stalker might have separated a weaker animal from the group before moving in for the kill.

IGUANODON

ALLOSAURUS SKULL

What was a killer's main weapon?

The large predator's ultimate weapon was its jaws. They were massive and incredibly powerful. Specially designed "windows" in the skull made it lightweight without losing strength. _Allosaurus_'s jaws were flexible, allowing it to open its mouth wide enough to swallow huge mouthfuls of flesh—perhaps even an entire creature.

How were curved
fangs used?

Predatory dinosaurs such as *T. rex* had teeth that
curved inward. These were designed to give the
predator a better grip on its victim. The angle of the
teeth prevented an animal from struggling while the
daggerlike points pierced its flesh. If a dinosaur lost
a tooth in battle or in an accident, a new one grew to
replace it.

WHY DO DINOSAURS' TEETH SURVIVE WELL AS FOSSILS?

Dinosaurs' teeth survive well as fossils because they are the hardest part of the body and least subject to decay.

TYRANNOSAURUS JAW

Curved teeth held prey in place

Was *T. rex* a scavenger?

With a reputation as the "king of the killers," *Tyrannosaurus rex* was the size of a house, as heavy as an elephant, and had teeth as long and sharp as carving knives. Yet some paleontologists have argued that this fearsome dinosaur was actually a scavenger, feasting only on animals that were already dead. Some of the dinosaur's features appear to be designed for hunting, others for scavenging. The most likely answer is that *T. rex* was both, killing live prey but also feeding on animal remains whenever it found them.

Meat and bones •

COULD
TINY
ARMS
GRAPPLE
WITH PREY?

All tyrannosaurs had small arms but *T. rex*'s were the tiniest for its size. For many years their purpose puzzled paleontologists. However, recent research suggests the arms were handy for hunting. The heavy arm bones, strong muscles, and limited range of movement would have made the arms the right tools for holding struggling prey.

Two-fingered hand with sharp claws

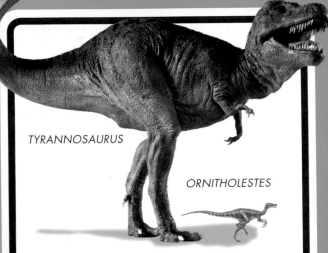

TYRANNOSAURUS

ORNITHOLESTES

HOW FAST WAS *T. REX*?

Most experts estimate the top speed at between 10-25 mph (16-40 km/h). Studies have shown that *T. rex*'s legs weren't strong enough to absorb the pounding of its 6 tons of body weight at faster speeds. However, although *T. rex* was slower than the fastest dinosaurs (such as *Ornitholestes*), it was fast enough to catch potential prey, such as lumbering plant-eater *Triceratops*.

How big was its bite?

T. rex had the biggest and the strongest jaws of any dinosaur—they could measure up to 4 ft (1.2 m) long. Experts estimate that *T. rex* could eat up to 500 lb (230 kg) of meat and bones in a single bite. This is strong evidence that the dinosaur was a hunter, for scavengers would not have needed such size or power.

TYRANNOSAURUS REX JAWS

Largest teeth were 9 in (23 cm) long

Hinge for opening lower jaw wide

DID *T. REX* HAVE GOOD EYESIGHT?

Strong vision is essential for hunting but less so for scavenging. *T. rex* had eyes that were angled forward, giving it some degree of binocular vision. This means that it could judge the distance of an object where the fields of view from its left eye and right eye overlapped. *T. rex*'s eyesight was probably good enough for stalking prey.

T. REX FIELD OF VIEW

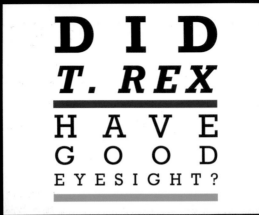

→ Field of view overlap

Left eye field of view

Right eye field of view

DO SCAVENGERS NEED A STRONG SENSE OF SMELL?

Prominent nostrils

Scavenging animals track down dead meat by following its smell, so a sensitive nose is essential. Experiments have shown that *T. rex* did have a heightened sense of smell—scans of the dinosaur's skull reveal exceptionally large olfactory lobes (smell detectors). But this alone is not enough to prove that it was a scavenger. A good sense of smell is an essential tool for hunting, too.

Did carnivores eat only **meat**?

Most people think of carnivorous dinosaurs sinking their teeth into a tasty plant-eater, which they certainly did. But they ate other animals, too. Recent evidence suggests that some dinosaurs preferred fish to meat, and others may have eaten both meat and plants. Fish-eating dinosaurs, such as *Suchomimus*, were built a little differently from their meat-eating cousins, with teeth designed for gripping their slippery prey. Dinosaur teeth provide basic information about diet, but paleontologists can discover more details from dinosaurs' fossilized droppings.

Long, narrow jaw with sharp teeth

SUCHOMIMUS

Curved thumb claw

Claw 12 in (30 cm) long

How did a dinosaur hook a fish?

At first, paleontologists were puzzled by *Baryonyx*'s long, curved thumb claw. After finding fish near the dinosaur's skeleton, which suggested that it was a fish-eater, they think they know what the dinosaur did with its claw. *Baryonyx* probably used it to hook fish out of the water, in much the same way that bears do.

Nostrils high on snout enabled dinosaur to breathe with its mouth in the water

SPINOSAURUS

HOW WERE FISH-EATERS LIKE
CROCODILES?

The long, narrow skulls of fish-eaters were more like the heads of crocodiles than those of other dinosaurs. The jaws were packed with about 100 pointed, serrated teeth. *Spinosaurus* may have dipped its long snout into the shallow waters of a lake or river to search for fish, then crunched them up with its many teeth.

Did any dinosaurs eat
MAMMALS?

Carnivores such as *Syntarsus* didn't prey on fellow dinosaurs. Instead, they made do with other animals. Mammals, such as the shrewlike *Megazostrodon*, would have made a tasty snack until a more satisfying meal could be found. Many theropods would also have eaten lizards, turtles, and eggs, including those of other dinosaurs.

SYNTARSUS

WERE THERE ANY DINOSAURS THAT ATE BOTH MEAT AND PLANTS?

Most dinosaurs were either carnivores, eating other animals, or herbivores, eating only plants, but a few were able to eat both. The name for these animals is omnivores. Omnivorous dinosaurs were small, birdlike theropods. Omnivore *Gallimimus* darted about the plains, picking off insects and lizards, and also munching on the vegetation.

GALLIMIMUS

COPROLITES
(DINOSAUR DUNG)

How do we know about dinosaur diets?

Fossilized dinosaur droppings, known as coprolites, can reveal valuable information about dinosaur diets. Pieces of bone found in a dropping may belong to another dinosaur or other animal; undigested plant matter may contain identifiable spores or pollen. Paleontologists can even figure out the shape of a dinosaur's intestines from the shape of the coprolite.

GIANTS Or

Small head

The most striking characteristic of the sauropods was their size, for they were the biggest animals to walk the Earth. Their body design did not vary as much as in other dinosaur groups—they all had large bodies and small heads, and most had very long necks and tails, like this *Brachiosaurus*. All the sauropods were herbivorous, maintaining their massive bodies with only plant matter. Like their enemies the theropods, the sauropods belonged to the lizard-hipped type of dinosaurs.

BRACHIOSAURUS

Big lungs

Shoulder joint

Elbow joint

Saurischian (lizard) hips

WHAT IS A SAUROPOD?

WHO WAS THE BIGGEST OF THEM ALL?

ARGENTINOSAURUS

Muscular tail

There are several contenders for this title. *Seismosaurus* and *Paralititan* were both giants among sauropods, but *Argentinosaurus* may have been the biggest. Although only a few bones of this dinosaur have been recovered, paleontologists have estimated its length at about 125 ft (37.5 m) and its weight at 80–100 tons. It is still possible that an even bigger sauropod may be discovered.

MAGYAROSAURUS

WERE THERE ANY SMALL SAUROPODS?

One of the smallest known sauropods measured 20 ft (6 m) from head to tail. *Magyarosaurus* and other smaller sauropods have been discovered in parts of Europe that were a group of islands in Cretaceous times. It is likely that the sauropods living there became smaller over thousands of years because of a limited food supply.

HOW LONG WAS THE LONGEST NECK?

The neck of an adult *Mamenchisaurus* was an incredible 46 ft (14 m) long. The neck was made up of 19 spinal bones (vertebrae), more than in any other dinosaur. The vertebrae were linked to one another by bony struts, which made the neck quite stiff. The vertebrae were hollow and thin to make the neck as lightweight as possible.

MAMENCHISAURUS

Neck held stiffly

Total length of dinosaur was 72 ft (22 m)

WHO HAD THE
LONGEST TAIL?

Diplodocus is the most likely holder of this title. This dinosaur had a tail measuring around 46 ft (14 m), as long as *Mamenchisaurus*'s neck. The tail was composed of about 80 vertebrae, which became narrower at the tail's tip. *Diplodocus* probably used its tail as a counterbalance for its long neck and it may have whipped attackers with its tail, too.

DIPLODOCUS

Did sauropods have thick skin?

Sauropods had thick skin for protection against attackers. However, these skin textures would have varied between groups. A section of fossilized skin from a *Saltasaurus*, above, has been discovered, showing bumpy skin inset with little bony plates. Other sauropods may have had smoother, more lizardlike skin. Some even had ridged spikes running along their backs.

Tail was thick at its base

WAS **BIGGER** ALWAYS BETTER?

As tens of millions of years passed, the sauropods and theropods grew ever larger. It seems that they were locked into an evolutionary size race—as the theropods became larger and more fierce, the sauropods grew bigger to counter any attack. In the end, sauropods such as *Camarasaurus* dwarfed *Allosaurus* and the other theropods. Being massive, however, had its disadvantages, such as lack of speed. Meanwhile, other plant-eating dinosaurs developed alternative methods of defense, often growing too tough or too nimble for theropods to tackle.

Sauropod is 75 ft (23 m) long

CAMARASAURUS

Theropod is 39 ft (12m) long

ALLOSAURUS

GARGOYLEOSAURUS

Stiff neck
ending in
small head

Were all the
plant-eaters huge?

Not all plant-eating dinosaurs became enormous in
response to the threat of theropods. *Gargoyleosaurus*
was 10–13 ft (3–4 m) long, one of the smallest of
the ankylosaur group. Although relatively small,
Gargoyleosaurus was capable of surviving an attack
by a theropod. Its vicious shoulder spikes and bony
back plates would have made it a tough meal.

Heart   *BRACHIOSAURUS*

Did sauropods have extra-powerful hearts?

Some experts think that the bigger sauropods, such as *Brachiosaurus*, may have needed large, powerful hearts and super-high blood pressure to pump blood around their massive bodies and up their necks to their brains. It is possible that they had hearts with four chambers, like humans and other mammals, rather than three chambers, like most reptiles.

WHAT DO FOSSIL FOOTPRINTS TELL US?

To estimate how fast a dinosaur moved, paleontologists examine the anatomy of the animal and, where available, its footprints. They can figure out its moving speed by measuring distance between the tracks— although footprints from a running dinosaur are very rare. These *Brontopodus* tracks indicate that the large sauropods had a top speed of about 6 mph (10 km/h).

BRONTOPODUS FOOTPRINTS

Strong leg bones

DIPLODOCUS FOREFOOT

ELEPHANT FOREFOOT

HOW DID SAUROPODS CARRY THEIR WEIGHT?

Experts once thought that sauropods lived in water because they would have been too heavy to support their own weight. Today, they agree that sauropods were designed to carry their weight, just as elephants are. Their legs were as sturdy as pillars and their toes, which splayed out to spread the weight, were cushioned by big pads of flesh. A large fleshy heel helped support the weight.

COULD A PLANT-EATER BE QUICK ON ITS FEET?

Not all plant-eaters were big or covered with body armor—some used their agility to escape danger. The ornithopod group of dinosaurs included lightly built animals such as *Dryosaurus*, which could run at high speeds. Like the theropods, *Dryosaurus* had a stiff tail for balancing as it sprinted on its hind legs.

DRYOSAURUS

Short arms with five-fingered hands

Long, lightly built legs

COULD
SALTASAURUS
REAR UP ON ITS
HIND LEGS?

1

Slightly longer hind legs meant that the dinosaur's weight could be shifted to the back of the animal.

The skeletons of *Saltasaurus* and some other sauropods suggest that they may have been able to rock back onto their hind legs and lift their front legs off the ground to reach foliage high up in the trees.

2

The tail acted as a third leg, providing extra stability as the dinosaur balanced on its two hind legs.

3

Once on its hind legs, the dinosaur's center of gravity was shifted to the back half of its huge body.

How did plant-eaters find food?

Plants common in the age of the dinosaurs included ginkgo trees, palmlike trees, coniferous trees, and ferns and mosses. It is likely that herbivorous dinosaurs ate all these plants. Different plant-eating dinosaurs developed different ways of breaking down their food. Sauropods, such as *Barosaurus*, raked foliage into their mouths with peglike teeth and swallowed it whole. It was then broken down in their digestive systems. Other plant-eating dinosaurs ground down plant matter with their teeth before swallowing.

BAROSAURUS

FOSSILIZED GINKGO

MODERN-DAY GINKGO

WHAT DID SAUROPODS EAT?

Their enormous size meant that sauropods had to spend nearly all their time eating just to generate enough energy to stay alive. They probably fed mostly on coniferous trees, steadily munching their way through entire forests. It is this continuous eating that may have created what is known as a "browse line," leaving trees bare of leaves below a certain level.

Were there flowers and grass?

Flowering plants first appeared in the early Cretaceous Period. Passion flowers, as well as flowering trees such as magnolia, beech, oak, maple, and walnut joined earlier plants. It is likely that dinosaurs ate the new flowers alongside leafy plant matter. Recent evidence from dinosaur droppings (coprolites) shows that some sauropods also munched on grass.

PASSION FLOWER

IGUANODON SKULL

Cheek teeth for grinding food

COULD A PLANT-EATER
chew its food?

Plant-eaters didn't have molars, like humans, and many could not chew. But some had toothless, horny beaks for snipping plants, as well as rows of teeth in their cheeks for grinding them down. Each tooth was coarsely serrated. Years of grinding tough plants wore teeth down. Those shown here are from an *Iguanodon*. One is in good condition; the other is worn.

LOWER TOOTH

WORN LOWER TOOTH

DID PLANT-EATERS
SWALLOW STONES?

These smooth stones, known as gastroliths, were recovered from the skeletons of various sauropods. Perhaps the dinosaurs had deliberately swallowed stones to aid their digestion. The stones might have stayed in a dinosaur's digestive system, grinding up the vegetation that it swallowed. However, it is more than likely that raw vegetation was broken down by special bacteria, as happens in the stomachs of cows.

GASTROLITHS

THECODONTOSAURUS

Neck suitable for browsing

WERE **LONG** NECKS USEFUL?

Long claws for hooking plants •

Some long-necked dinosaurs probably lifted their heads to reach high up in the trees. Others, such as this *Thecodontosaurus*, may also have used them to reach into the middle of low-growing plants. *Thecodontosaurus* was a likely ancestor of the sauropods and had a much shorter neck than its later relatives.

WHERE DID PLANT-EATERS LIVE?

PARALITITAN

During the 160 million years that dinosaurs existed, new landmasses appeared and different habitats were created. The herbivores, along with carnivores, lived in most of them, although tropical forest was a favored habitat for big sauropods. Some plant-eaters adapted to extreme conditions, while others may have moved on to find new lands. Whether in a forest or a windswept plain, many of the herbivores spent their lives with each other, perhaps even living in herds of thousands.

How had the landscape changed?

By the Cretaceous Period, the world's landmass was splitting into continents, which looked closer to those that we recognize today. New groups of dinosaurs arose in different places. The horned dinosaurs, for example, emerged in Asia, but crossed into North America, where they were able to flourish.

CRETACEOUS EARTH

EUROPE

NORTH AMERICA

TETHYS SEA

ASIA

AFRICA

INDIA

SOUTH AMERICA

AUSTRALIA

ANTARCTICA

DID SAUROPODS LIVE TOGETHER?

Evidence suggests that many types of plant-eating dinosaurs, including sauropods such as *Barosaurus*, lived together in herds. Being part of a group usually gives an individual animal greater protection against predators. It is also possible that sauropods were sociable animals. A herd may have contained a number of family groups that roamed the countryside together.

BAROSAURUS

CORYTHOSAURUS

Who chose to live near swamps?

Fossils of *Corythosaurus* and other hadrosaurs (sometimes called duck-billed dinosaurs) have been discovered in rocks that were laid down in swamps. People once supposed that the hadrosaurs fed on water plants that grew in swamps, like the modern North American moose. Experts now believe hadrosaurs spent most of their time on dry land.

METHODS

HOW DID PLANT-EATERS
FIGHT BACK?

To defend themselves against predators, the different plant-eating dinosaurs developed an impressive armory of weapons. The ankylosaur *Euoplocephalus* had a ball of thickened bone at the end of its tail, which it could swing at attackers. The stegosaurs had tails studded with daggerlike spikes for stabbing attackers, while the sauropods' size was their main defense. Some dinosaurs had features that puzzle paleontologists, because it is unclear whether they were weapons or merely tools for feeding.

Flexible armored bands

EUOPLOCEPHALUS

Pointed scutes (bony plates) ran in rows

Toothless beak

Sturdy legs

WHICH DINOSAURS HAD A
DISPLAY OF SPIKES?

A group of dinosaurs called stegosaurs are characterized by their spiked tails and plated backs. *Huayangosaurus* was an early stegosaur, living some 20 million years before its more famous American relative *Stegosaurus*. It may have used its tail spikes to deter attack from larger carnivores.

Muscular tail

Thickened bone

COULD A SAUROPOD CRUSH AN ATTACKER?

A big sauropod, such as *Barosaurus*, had one decisive weapon against even the largest theropods—sheer weight. Its 20-ton body could easily crush the bones and suck the air from the lungs of a 3-ton *Allosaurus*. *Barosaurus* may have resorted to crushing attackers in extreme circumstances, such as to protect its young.

BAROSAURUS

• Strong, thin tail

ALLOSAURUS

How useful were massive claws?

Therizinosaurus had three huge, lethal-looking claws on each hand. However, some experts think the claws were too blunt to be used as weapons. Instead, they may have been used for feeding—to pluck foliage from trees or to rip open the nests of termites. If so, how this dinosaur defended itself remains a mystery.

THERIZINOSAURUS

WHICH WAS THE
SPIKIEST
DINOSAUR?

Kentrosaurus, meaning "spiked lizard," was certainly one
of the spikiest. It was an East African stegosaur, which
measured about 16 ft (5 m) long. Pairs of bone plates
protected its neck, shoulders, and back. Six pairs of spikes—
each of which was up to 2 ft (60 cm) in length—adorned
its lower back and tail. *Kentrosaurus* would have used these
spikes to fend off theropods, such as *Allosaurus*.

Protective spikes

KENTROSAURUS

WHICH DINOSAUR HAD A
THUMB SPIKE?

Iguanodon was a large herbivore without spines, plates, or claws. Its only defensive weapon was a single long spike on each thumb. Paleontologists believe this dinosaur may have jabbed at attacking theropods with the spike. *Iguanodon* had unusually flexible hands and was able to grasp food in its fingers.

Thumb spike up to 6 in (15 cm) in length

IGUANODON

DID BODY **ARMOR** REALLY HELP?

Many dinosaurs had some protective armor, but the ankylosaurs were the most heavily armored of all. Some were covered in a mosaic of bony plates and studs, and many bristled with spines and spikes, too. Only their bellies were unprotected, and ankylosaurs may have crouched to avoid exposing them when attacked. It would have taken a hungry theropod to tackle spiky *Gastonia*, which may have responded by driving its shoulder spines into its attacker's leg.

WHAT WAS THE ARMOR MADE OF?

The flat plates embedded in the skin of the ankylosaurs are known as scutes by paleontologists. The ankylosaurs' armor of scutes, studs, and spikes was made of hardened bone, sometimes covered in horn. *Edmontonia* had scutes around its shoulders and along its tail, as well as triangular spikes on its back.

Curved dorsal spines

Broad, flat spikes

GASTONIA

Horny, toothless beak

WHAT WAS A NASAL BOSS?

One of the horned dinosaurs, *Pachyrhinosaurus*, has a name that means "thick-nosed lizard." On its nose—where its cousins had a sharp horn—*Pachyrhinosaurus* had a big bony knob. This was the nasal boss. Rival family members may have scrapped with each other, using their nasal bosses as weapons.

Lump of thick bone

PACHYRHINOSAURUS

ANKYLOSAUR
SKIN

Who had bulletproof skin?

Recent research has shown that the skin on the backs and tails of some of the ankylosaurs was virtually bulletproof—and certainly tooth-proof. The big scutes, smaller irregular plates, and the hexagonal plates interlocked to make the skin so tough and light that experts have likened it to fiberglass.

WHICH DINOSAUR WAS BONE-HEADED?

Pachycephalosaurus was an ugly beast. It had a dome-shaped head edged with horny bumps, and several short bony spikes on its nose. The dome was made of solid bone, which was a whopping 10 in (25 cm) thick. *Pachycephalosaurus* may have used its head as a battering ram against attacking predators—or each other.

PACHYCEPHALOSAURUS

Were any sauropods ARMORED?

SALTASAURUS

Bony scutes •

• Shorter neck than other sauropods

Smaller lumps •

Although most of the sauropods relied on their size to defend themselves, some of them were lightly armored, too. *Saltasaurus* had two types of armor. Its back and neck were covered in fist-sized bony scutes, and much smaller lumps toughened the skin all over its body.

Were frills defensive?

The plated and horned groups of dinosaurs developed some impressive features. They had great frills edged with studs and spikes around their heads, or triangular plates of skin and bone along their backs. Some were used in fighting. But experts believe that some dinosaur features were just for display. Like a peacock's colorful fan of feathers, a male *Pentaceratops*'s head frill may have been used to help it attract a mate.

Large neck frill

PENTACERATOPS

Plain, bulky body

STYRACOSAURUS
SKULL

WHICH DINOSAUR HAD THE SPIKIEST FRILL?

Styracosaurus was one of the most spectacular looking of the horned dinosaurs. Its head broadened into a large frill that covered the back of its neck. Six long spikes flared from the top of the frill, and the sides were edged with studs. *Styracosaurus* also had a big horn on its snout, but seemingly no horns above its eyes.

Could a **skull** be a battering ram?

Triceratops, or "three-horned face," had a short nose horn and two long horns above its eyes. Its neck frill was edged with bony studs. About 50 *Triceratops* skulls have been discovered, and many of them show scarring. This is strong evidence that the dinosaur used its tough skull as a weapon against larger predators.

TRICERATOPS SKULL

Horns

Eye socket

Did horned dinosaurs
FIGHT
EACH OTHER?

The horned dinosaurs would have fought off attacking theropods, but they probably also clashed with each other. They may have crashed their heads together, damaging each other's frills with their horns and spikes, or locked horns and shoved. Such battles would have been fought over territory or potential mates.

STYRACOSAURUSES

Large,
bony plates

STEGOSAURUS

WHAT WERE
STEGOSAURUS'S
PLATES FOR?

The bony plates running along *Stegosaurus*'s back were
almost certainly not weapons. Experts think they were
covered in skin, making them quite soft, with blood
vessels (veins) inside. If this is correct, the plates
may have helped to regulate body temperature.
They would have absorbed the Sun's
heat, warming up *Stegosaurus*.

WHICH DINOSAUR HAD A MAIN SAIL?

The big carnivore *Spinosaurus* had spines up to 6 ft (2 m) long along its back. These were connected by skin, making the feature look like a sail. This sail may have helped *Spinosaurus* keep cool in the hot African climate, or simply been used for display—to attract a mate.

SPINOSAURUS

How did dinosaurs ESCAPE DANGER?

When threatened, animals will try to avoid a fight, and dinosaurs probably behaved much like other animals. *Gallimimus* was one of the fastest dinosaurs, possibly sprinting at speeds of up to 50 mph (80 km/h) to outrun predators. Other dinosaurs found different ways to keep out of harm's way. Some developed skin that was colored and patterned to blend in with their environments. Others kept to the safety of the herd. A few dinosaurs could even make sounds that signaled the approach of danger.

GALLIMIMUS

Long tail for balance while running

Flexible neck

Tube of
nasal bones

HOW DID DINOSAURS SOUND OUT A WARNING?

Duck-billed dinosaur *Parasaurolophus* may have used its skull to communicate with other dinosaurs. The unusual crest on this dinosaur's head consisted of tubes connected to its nostrils. By blowing through its crest and nose, *Parasaurolophus* could have made a trumpeting noise, perhaps to warn that predators were nearby.

Birdlike beak

Feathers attached
to bony tail •

• Lightly
built body

Claws
on wing

ARCHAEOPTERYX

COULD
ANY DINOSAURS
FLY AWAY?

Dinosaurs are usually described as land animals, but one
species became so birdlike that it was able to fly. Experts
are not sure whether to describe *Archaeopteryx* as a bird
or a dinosaur. It was certainly capable of flying from
danger, but unlike modern birds it had teeth, a bony
tail, and clawed wings.

TRICERATOPS

WAS THERE SAFETY IN NUMBERS?

Dinosaurs living in herds would probably have been much safer than those that lived alone. If a herd of *Triceratops* was being stalked by a predator, for example, the adults could threaten to charge, while keeping their young well inside the group. *Triceratops* may also have been able to run at speeds of 15 mph (25 km/h).

OF AN ERA

WHAT KILLED THE DINOSAURS?

Some 65 million years ago, a catastrophic event occurred that wiped out more than half of all life on Earth, including the dinosaurs. Most experts believe this mass extinction was caused by an enormous asteroid crashing into the Earth. So much dust was blasted into the atmosphere that day became night for months on end and the temperatures plummeted. Close to the impact site the landscape was devastated, and dying dinosaurs would have stumbled around looking in vain for food and shelter.

TRICERATOPS WAS ONE OF THE LAST SURVIVORS

WHAT IS AN
asteroid?

An asteroid is a rocky object—smaller than a planet—that orbits the Sun. Every so often, their orbits bring some asteroids crashing into the Earth's surface. Although most are too small to cause long-term damage, the massive asteroid that probably caused the Cretaceous mass extinction made a crater 112 miles (180 km) wide.

ASTEROID IMPACT

WHAT ELSE MIGHT HAVE HAPPENED?

No one can be sure that an asteroid collision alone was the cause of the dinosaurs' extinction. Scientists also think that at the end of the Cretaceous Period there were numerous volcanic eruptions in India. These might have polluted the atmosphere with so much dust that the Sun's rays could not penetrate, and many creatures may have died of cold.

ERUPTING VOLCANO

PTERODACTYLUS

Did flying reptiles all die?

Throughout the time of the dinosaurs, the skies were filled with flying reptiles, but no pterosaurs survived the mass extinction. Reptiles would never take to the skies again and no human would see a *Pterodactylus* or a *Quetzalcoatlus*, the largest flying animal ever, swooping overhead.

WHAT HAPPENED TO MARINE ANIMALS?

When seas still teemed with life, the most dominant groups of sea creatures were the dinosaurs' distant relatives, marine reptiles. Like the dinosaurs, the marine reptiles, such as *Mosasaurus*, were all killed in the extinction event. Many other sea creatures died out or were seriously diminished, although fish were mostly unaffected.

WHICH MEAT-EATERS WERE THE LAST SURVIVORS?

The big theropod *T. rex* was among the last meat-eating dinosaurs to walk the Earth. After the asteroid impact, dead and dying animals would have been plentiful, so it is unlikely *T. rex* died of hunger. It is possible that, together with other dinosaurs, *T. rex* died out because the low temperatures made all hatchlings the same gender.

TYRANNOSAURUS REX

WHO WAS TOP PREDATOR
AFTER *T. REX*?

It was millions of years before big animals reappeared
following the mass extinction. While the dinosaurs were
alive, mammals remained relatively small, but they
gradually evolved to replace dinosaurs as the dominant
land animals. Hoofed beast *Andrewsarchus* became the
biggest carnivorous land mammal ever. However, these
large mammals faced competition from an unlikely
source when birds also evolved
into fierce predators.

ANDREWSARCHUS

PHENACODUS

WHAT DID
PREDATORY MAMMALS
EAT?

Andrewsarchus would have been able to hunt down plant-eating mammals, resembling this early hoofed herbivore called *Phenacodus*. About the size of a sheep, *Phenacodus* was lightly built so it stood some chance of escaping a predator. It probably lived in herds and kept to forests for feeding and shelter.

WHEN DID BIG PLANT-EATERS REAPPEAR?

Some 20 million years after the mass extinction, big plant-eating animals were back on the scene. *Uintatherium* was about the size and shape of a rhinoceros and had pillarlike, weight-bearing legs. It had three pairs of horns on its head and tusklike canine teeth, which it probably used for fighting. *Uintatherium* lived on a diet of leaves and fruit.

UINTATHERIUM

AMBULOCETUS

DID EARLY MAMMALS
LIVE IN WATER?

This animal looks like an otter, but was, in fact, a very early whale. Although *Ambulocetus* could walk on dry land, it was also a powerful swimmer, showing how whales evolved from land-dwelling mammals. It would take about 10 million years before watery mammals, such as *Ambulocetus*, evolved into the whales that we recognize today.

Massive beak for tearing flesh

WHICH BIRDS WERE PREDATORS?

Large, carnivorous, flightless birds became some of the world's fiercest predators. *Titanis*, or "terror bird," was about 7 ft (2 m) tall and had a sharp, hooked beak and huge claws. *Titanis* hunted small mammals on North America's open plains, where it competed with the big carnivorous mammals to be top predator.

TITANIS

Claws for seizing prey

ICARONYCTERIS

Large ears for hearing high-frequency sounds

WHEN DID
BATS
FIRST APPEAR?

Ten million years after the disappearance of the pterosaurs, the first flying mammals appeared. Bats have changed little since then and are still the only flying mammals. Many bats are nocturnal and use their special sense of hearing to find their way and locate prey in the dark.

WHICH ANIMALS ARE AS OLD AS DINOSAURS?

Even though dinosaurs were around for 160 million years, other animals have survived for as long, or even longer. Ancient animals live everywhere—on land, in the sky, and in the seas and rivers. Many of them have changed little from their prehistoric forms—crocodilians have not needed to adapt since Cretaceous times. If their habitats are preserved, these animals could continue living for millions more years.

CROCODILE

Short, sturdy limbs

Heavily armored skin

Feet designed for running on land

WHICH ARE THE MOST SUCCESSFUL ANIMALS?

Delicate wings strengthened by fine veins

DRAGONFLY

Insects are the most numerous and diverse animals that have ever existed on Earth. There are millions of different insect species and some of them have existed, relatively unchanged, since before the time of the dinosaurs. The oldest dragonfly fossil ever found is about 320 million years old, and dragonflies are still a common sight today.

IGUANA

Scaly skin
typical of lizards

DID ANY LAND REPTILES SURVIVE THE EXTINCTION?

Small lizards lived throughout the Mesozoic Era, and they are still with us today. Paleontologists are not sure why these reptiles were unaffected by whatever killed the dinosaurs. It is possible that when many plants had died, lizards burrowed into the ground and hibernated to escape the hazardous surface conditions.

HOW ANCIENT ARE ARACHNIDS?

Fossil evidence suggests that arachnids—the animal group that includes spiders and scorpions—are more than 400 million years old. There are hundreds of thousands of species today. All of them are predators, killing by injecting deadly chemicals, called venom, into their prey. The venom of some scorpions can kill humans.

Venom is injected from the tail

SCORPION

GREAT WHITE
SHARK

Which are the oldest sea creatures?

Marine invertebrates (animals without backbones),
including clams and jellyfish, are the oldest.
However, the most ancient big sea animal is
undoubtedly the shark. These formidable creatures
have survived more than 400 million years of history,
including the Cretaceous extinction.

Tough shell protects soft body parts

COCKROACH

Are cockroaches INDESTRUCTIBLE?

Cockroaches could be the most hardy of all insects. They eat almost anything, but they can also survive without food for about a month. They can even recover after being frozen. Cockroaches live everywhere except the polar regions. They have existed for 300 million years.

WHAT IS A
crocodilian?

This is the name for a group of archosaurs made up of crocodiles and their relatives. The first crocodilians appeared about the same time as the dinosaurs and lived on land. Soon, they evolved to live in oceans and rivers. Today, there are 23 crocodilian species.

GEOSAURUS

Geosaurus was an aquatic crocodilian of the Jurassic Period.

DEINOSUCHUS

At about 50 ft (15 m) in length, *Deinosuchus* was one of the biggest crocodilians. Its powerful jaws could probably crush a large dinosaur.

Instead of the heavy armor that most crocodilians have, *Geosaurus* had smooth skin, making it a more agile swimmer than its relatives.

Are **BIRDS** related to **DINOSAURS?**

A heron may not look like a dinosaur, but striking similarities exist between birds and dinosaurs. In recent years, new evidence has confirmed the link between them. Dinosaur fossils have been found that prove some species had distinctly birdlike features, and bird fossils have shown that the earliest birds had dinosaurlike attributes, too. Paleontologists think that a particular group of dinosaurs evolved into the thousands of bird species that exist today. Though we will never see a living dinosaur, we can see their descendants in the skies above us.

HERON

COMPSOGNATHUS

Stiff tail

Jaw lined
with sharp
teeth

Which dinosaurs do birds come from?

Paleontologists think birds evolved from a group of small, nimble, carnivorous theropods called maniraptorans. Members of this group, such as *Compsognathus*, are characterized by several birdlike features, including long legs and feet. Most importantly, they seized prey with arms that worked very much like wings.

HOW ARE DINOSAUR AND BIRD BONES SIMILAR?

Like birds, many dinosaurs had lightweight bones. Most animals have sturdy bones, but the bones of some dinosaurs and pterosaurs contained air-filled cavities to lessen the creature's weight. This was a vital asset for flying. There is another remarkable similarity—the skeletons of early birds and some theropods are almost identical.

LIGHTWEIGHT BIRD BONE

Claws attached to wings

CONFUCIUSORNIS

When did the first true bird appear?

Confuciusornis was the first known bird to have a horny toothless beak, like modern birds, although it still had dinosaurlike claws on its wing feathers. It appeared in Cretaceous China about 120 million years ago. Experts believe it had a different flying technique from that of birds today. Its large toes suggest that it could probably walk and climb, too.

WHICH DINOSAUR LOOKS LIKE A BIRD?

SHUVUUIA

• Body shape similar to a modern bird

When its fossil was discovered in 1998, experts debated whether *Shuvuuia* was a birdlike dinosaur or a dinosaurlike bird. Despite its birdlike features, including a coat of downy feathers, most paleontologists identified *Shuvuuia* as a member of a distinct group of theropod dinosaurs, characterized by their short, powerful arms. *Shuvuuia* may have used its arms to rip open termite nests.

INSECT PRESERVED
IN AMBER

COULD DINOSAURS EVER RETURN?

In the 1993 film *Jurassic Park*, experts brought dinosaurs back to life with dinosaur DNA taken from the body of a mosquito preserved in amber. In reality, any dinosaur DNA would almost certainly be too small a sample and too broken up to recreate a dinosaur. However, technology is always improving and dinosaur fossils are still being discovered...

FACTS

The word *dinosaur* means **"terrible lizard"** and was first used in 1842.

The birdlike *Microraptor* is one of the smallest dinosaurs yet discovered— it was just 30 in (77 cm) long. The remains were found in a lake bed in China in 2000.

Deinosuchus,

a huge alligator, was capable of feasting on large dinosaurs. This massive, river-dwelling reptile's skull alone measured 6 ft (1.8 m).

Dinosaurs could be born as **IDENTICAL TWINS** or even as TRIPLETS.

Tyrannosaurus rex

would have needed about **300 lb** (136 kg) **of meat** each day to keep it supplied with energy.

Some paleontologists think that *T. rex* may have had feathers.

As plant-eaters' **teeth** wore down, new ones grew to replace them.

Duck-billed dinosaur *Edmontosaurus* had about **1,000 teeth** in its cheeks, more than any other dinosaur.

Sauropods were more comfortable in forest habitats because the trees shaded their huge bodies from the Sun.

Dinosaur fossils often show evidence of fighting in the form of broken bones.

Among the first dinosaur fossils to be studied were those of the plant-eater *Iguanodon*.

The plant-eating dinosaur *Protoceratops* had a neck frill, but the males had much bigger frills than the females. This supports the idea that frills attracted females.

THE HEAD OF *STYRACOSAURUS* WAS TALLER THAN AN AVERAGE-SIZED MAN!

ONE EARLY THEORY SUGGESTED THAT THE DINOSAURS' EXTINCTION WAS CAUSED BY MAMMALS EATING all their eggs.

Many bird groups evolved, including modern ones, such as **owls, swifts, herons, and eagles.**

In the far distant past only about one bird species became extinct every century, but today the rate is about **100 times that.**

INDEX

CREDITS

The publisher would like to thank the following for their kind permission to reproduce their photographs:

Key: a=above; b=below/bottom; c=center; l=left; r=right; t=top.

Alamy Images: Mediacolor's 90t (b/g). **Corbis:** Gunter Marx Photography 68-69 (b/g); Alfio Scigliano/Sygma 122b. **DK Images:** American Museum of Natural History 98b, 109tr; Bedrock Studios 8, 22, 33, 76-77, 81, 130, 131; Robert L. Braun—modelmaker 1t, 5, 27cl (stegosaurus), 20, 104, 112, 111, 141; Centaur Studios—modelmakers 26-27b (baryonyx), 101r; Jonathan Hately—modelmaker 62-63; Graham High at Centaur Studios—modelmaker 2, 1b, 19tr, 27bc (triceratops), 57tr, 61, 58tc, 114-115b, 117; Jeremy Hunt at Centaur Studios—modelmaker 6bl, 9, 84; Museo Arentino De Cirendas Naterales, Buenos Aires 75; Natural History Museum, London 3, 16, 18-19b, 39, 43l, 48, 54-55, 74-75, 105, 110; Peabody Museum of Natural History, Yale University 51b; State Museum of Nature, Stuttgart 14, 36b, 53; Dennis Wilson—Staab Studios 108bl, 108br; Jerry Young 132. **Getty Images:** Science Faction/Louie Psihoyos 79. **Natural Visions:** Richard Coomber/Heather Angel 114-115b (b/g). **Natural History Museum, London:** 17. naturepl.com: Pete Oxford 140-141b. **Science Photo Library:** David A. Hardy, Futures: 50 Years In Space 121; S. R. Maglione 108 (b/g).

Jacket images: Front: **DK Images:** Jon Hughes/ Bedrock Studios. Back: **DK Images:** Natural History Museum, London bl.

All other images © Dorling Kindersley
For further information see: **www.dkimages.com**